TRUMPET
TRUMPET
TRUMPET
TRUMPET
TRUMPET
TRUMPET
TRUMPET

From JC…

Welcome to the first ever, inter-galactically celebrated, JC & the Mu'tet Play Along! I hope that one day, these tunes might be played all over the universe on space instruments! Featured on this is my group, the Mu'tet - Roy 'Futureman' Wooten (from Bela Fleck & the Flecktones) on drums, Felix Pastorius (formerly with the Yellow Jackets and son of the legendary Jaco Pastorius) on electric bass, Chris Walters on piano/keys and Bill 'the Spaceman' Fanning on trumpet.

I chose some of my original tunes for this first play along that I thought would provide the most benefits. My thought was to include fun tunes that present challenges but that are easily playable and at tempos that the players can really learn something from. So, I hope that you have fun playing this music and that you learn something along the way too.

On certain tunes, I thought it a good idea to have us 'trade fours' with you on a chorus or two after the given solo section. There are a few options for each track and you can choose if you want horns, no horns, backgrounds, melody, etc…I hope to eventually make these even more interactive so stay tuned! Each tune will have the various options listed for you to choose from.

There are also full versions of two tunes, *Come On Up* & *Uncle Salty*, which were previously unrecorded and unreleased. I wanted you to hear these incredible musicians in the Mu'tet and hear how we play together and listen to one another.

Other than *Come on Up* & *Uncle Salty*, all the tunes have been previously recorded and released. I highly encourage you to check out the original versions! Go to **www.jeffcoffin.com** for links to listen or buy.

As mentioned previously, all of the tunes have a few different versions to play to. I think it's important for you to hear how we play the melodies and to hear the 'landmarks' in regards to backgrounds, and sometimes other internal phrases, as you are playing. Imitation is a big part of learning, but, eventually, you have to find your own way through.

I tried to give a wide musical variety of tunes in style and feel and I wanted to make it very accessible to you as listeners. Melody, harmony and rhythm are very important fundamental elements in music and I feel these tunes carry strong components of each.

I hope you get as much enjoyment playing this music as we do. Feel free to play them on gigs and to encourage others to check them out. This play along is for YOU to enjoy and learn from. I hope you do both!!

Peace, JC

P.S. Been mu'tated…lately?

Quick Reference Guide

TRACK	TITLE	TRACK INFO
Track 1	**Come On Up**	Melody/Backgrounds
Track 2	Come On Up	Melody/Backgrounds/Trades
Track 3	Come On Up	Backgrounds only
Track 4	Come On Up	No Horns
Track 5	**A Joe Jones**	Melody/Backgrounds
Track 6	A Joe Jones	Melody/Backgrounds/Trades
Track 7	A Joe Jones	Backgrounds only
Track 8	A Joe Jones	No Horns
Track 9	**Uncle Salty**	Melody/Backgrounds
Track 10	Uncle Salty	Backgrounds only
Track 11	Uncle Salty	No Horns
Track 12	**Al's Greens**	Melody/Backgrounds
Track 13	Al's Greens	Backgrounds only
Track 14	Al's Greens	No Horns
Track 15	**Espoo You**	Melody/Backgrounds
Track 16	Espoo You	Melody/Backgrounds/Trades
Track 17	Espoo You	Backgrounds only
Track 18	Espoo You	No Horns
Track 19	**The Mad Hatter Rides Again** (mm 120)	Melody/ Backgrounds
Track 20	The Mad Hatter Rides Again (mm 120)	Backgrounds only
Track 21	The Mad Hatter Rides Again (mm 120)	No Horns
Track 22	**Steppin' Up**	Melody/Backgrounds
Track 23	Steppin' Up	Melody/Backgrounds/Trades
Track 24	Steppin' Up	Backgrounds only
Track 25	Steppin' Up	No Horns
Track 26	**Tall & Lanky**	Melody/Backgrounds
Track 27	Tall & Lanky	Backgrounds only
Track 28	Tall & Lanky	No Horns
Track 29	**The Mad Hatter Rides Again** (mm 137)	Melody/Backgrounds
Track 30	The Mad Hatter Rides Again (mm 137)	Backgrounds only
Track 31	The Mad Hatter Rides Again (mm 137)	No Horns
Track 32	**Sweet Magnolias**	Melody/Backgrounds
Track 33	Sweet Magnolias	No Horns
Track 34	**Move Your Rug**	Melody/Backgounds
Track 35	Move Your Rug	Melody/Backgrounds/Trades
Track 36	Move Your Rug	Backgrounds only
Track 37	Move Your Rug	No Horns
Track 38	Come On Up	**Full Version**
Track 39	Uncle Salty	**Full Version**

01) COME ON UP

Track 1
(melody/bgds)
melody 1x
solo section 5x
bgds 2nd, 4th, 5th x's
melody 1x

Track 2
(melody/bgds/trades)
melody 1x
solo section 4x
bgds 2nd, 4th x's
trades 1x
melody 1x

Track 3
(bgds only)
melody 1x
solo section 5x
bgds 2nd, 4th, 5th x's
melody 1x

Track 4
(no horns)
melody 1x
solo section 5x
bgds 2nd, 4th, 5th x's
melody 1x

02) A JOE JONES

Track 5
(melody/bgds)
melody 2x
solo section 6x
melody 2x

Track 6
(melody/bgds/trades)
melody 2x
solo section 4x
trades 2x
melody 2x

Track 7
(bgds only)
melody 2x
solo section 6x
melody 2x

Track 8
(no horns)
melody 2x
solo section 6x
melody 2x

03) UNCLE SALTY

Track 9
(melody/bgds)
melody
solo section (watch your repeats)
melody 1x

Track 10
(bgds only)
melody
solo section (watch your repeats)
melody 1x

Track 11
(no horns)
melody
solo section (watch your repeats)
melody 1x

04) AL'S GREENS

Track 12
(melody/bgds)
intro
melody 2x
solo section (AAB) 2x
melody 1x

Track 13
(bgds only)
intro
melody 2x
solo section (AAB) 2x
melody 1x

Track 14
(no horns)
intro
melody 2x
solo section (AAB) 2x
melody 1x

05) ESPOO YOU

Track 15
(melody/bgds)
melody 1x
solo section 3x
melody 1x
to coda

Track 16
(melody/bgds/trades)
melody 1x
solo section 2x
trades 1x
melody 1x
to coda

Track 17
(bgds only)
melody 1x
solo section 3x
melody 1x
to coda

Track 18
(no horns)
melody 1x
solo section 3x
melody 1x
to coda

06) THE MAD HATTER RIDES AGAIN (120 bpm)

Track 19
(melody/bgds)
read chart as written
solo at C.

Track 20
(bgds only)
read chart as written
solo at C.

Track 21
(no horns)
read chart as written
solo at C.

07) STEPPIN' UP

Track 22
(melody/bgds)
intro - 8 bars drums
melody 1x (AAB)
solo section 3x (AAB)
Melody 1x (one A ONLY)

Track 23
(melody/bgds/trades)
intro - 8 bars drums
melody 1x (AAB)
solo section 2x (AAB)
trades 1x (AAB)
Melody 1x (one A ONLY)

Track 24
(bgds only)
intro - 8 bars drums
melody 1x (AAB)
solo section 3x (AAB)
Melody 1x (one A ONLY)

Track 25
(no horns)
intro - 8 bars drums
melody 1x (AAB)
solo section 3x (AAB)
Melody 1x (one A ONLY)

08) TALL & LANKY

Track 26
(melody/bgds)
intro
melody 2x
solo section 6x
melody 2x

Track 27
(bgds only)
intro
melody 2x
solo section 6x
melody 2x

Track 28
(no horns)
intro
melody 2x
solo section 6x
melody 2x

09) THE MAD HATTER RIDES AGAIN (137 bpm)

Track 29
(melody/bgds)
read chart as written
(2 solos-DS back to B. for 2nd solo)

Track 30
(bgds only)
read chart as written
(2 solos-DS back to B. for 2nd solo)

Track 31
(no horns)
read chart as written
(2 solos-DS back to B. for 2nd solo)

10) SWEET MAGNOLIAS

Track 32
(melody/bgds)
melody 1x
solo section 1 1/2 x
melody at B. to fine

Track 33
(no horns)
melody 1x
solo section 1 1/2 x
melody at B. to fine

11) MOVE YOUR RUG

Track 34
(melody/bgds)
intro - 8 bars drums
melody 1x (AABA)
solo section 3x
(bgds at C. 2nd & 3rd x)
melody 1x to CODA

Track 35
(melody/bgds/trades)
intro - 8 bars drums
melody 1x (AABA)
solo section 2x
(bgds at C. 2nd x)
trades 1x (bgds at C.)
melody 1x (AABA) to CODA

Track 36
(bgds only)
intro - 8 bars drums
melody 1x (AABA)
solo section 3x
(bgds at C. 2nd & 3rd x)
melody 1x to CODA

Track 37
(no horns)
intro - 8 bars drums
melody 1x (AABA)
solo section 3x
(bgds at C. 2nd & 3rd x)
melody 1x to CODA

JEFF COFFIN & the MU'TET
Play Along / Volume 1

JC & the MU'TET
Jeff Coffin – Soprano/Alto/Tenor Sax
Roy 'Futureman' Wooten – Drums/Percussion
Felix Pastorius – Electric Bass
Bill Fanning – Trumpet
Chris Walters – Piano/Hammond B-3/Wurlitzer Electric Piano

Recorded May 4, 2014 @ Blackbird Studio D / Nashville, TN
Produced by Jeff Coffin
Engineer: Nate 'Pittsburgh' Dickinson
Assistant Engineer: Lowell Reynolds
Studio Assistant: Alex Clayton
Mixed by Nate Dickinson
Mastered by Jim Demain / Yes Mastering, Nashville, TN

All Compositions by Jeff Coffin
Otani Music/BMI

Jeff Coffin plays Yamaha Saxophones & D'Addario Reeds
Roy Wooten plays Sleishman Drums & Sabian Cymbals
Felix Pastorius plays Fodera Basses

Special thanks to John Hinchey for his invaluable help on Sibelius and to the Mu'tet for everything they do. Thanks to Nate Dickinson for all his hard work on the mixes and to my Yamaha and D'Addario families for their continued support of music education. To my students and teachers, you have taught me so much, this is for you!

As always, my biggest thanks goes to my incredible wife, Ryoko, for putting up with my continued musical insanity. :)

For more info or to contact Jeff, please visit:
www.jeffcoffin.com
www.earuprecords.com

Track 1 (melody/bgds) melody 1x solo section 5x bgds 2nd, 4th, 5th x's melody 1x	Track 2 (melody/bgds/trades) melody 1x solo section 4x bgds 2nd, 4th x's trades 1x melody 1x	Track 3 (bgds only) melody 1x solo section 5x bgds 2nd, 4th, 5th x's melody 1x	Track 4 (no horns) melody 1x solo section 5x bgds 2nd, 4th, 5th x's melody 1x

Trumpet in B♭

A JOE JONES

Composed by Jeff Coffin

Track 5-Melody & BGs
Track 6-Melody, BGs, Trades
Track 7-BGs
Track 8-No horns

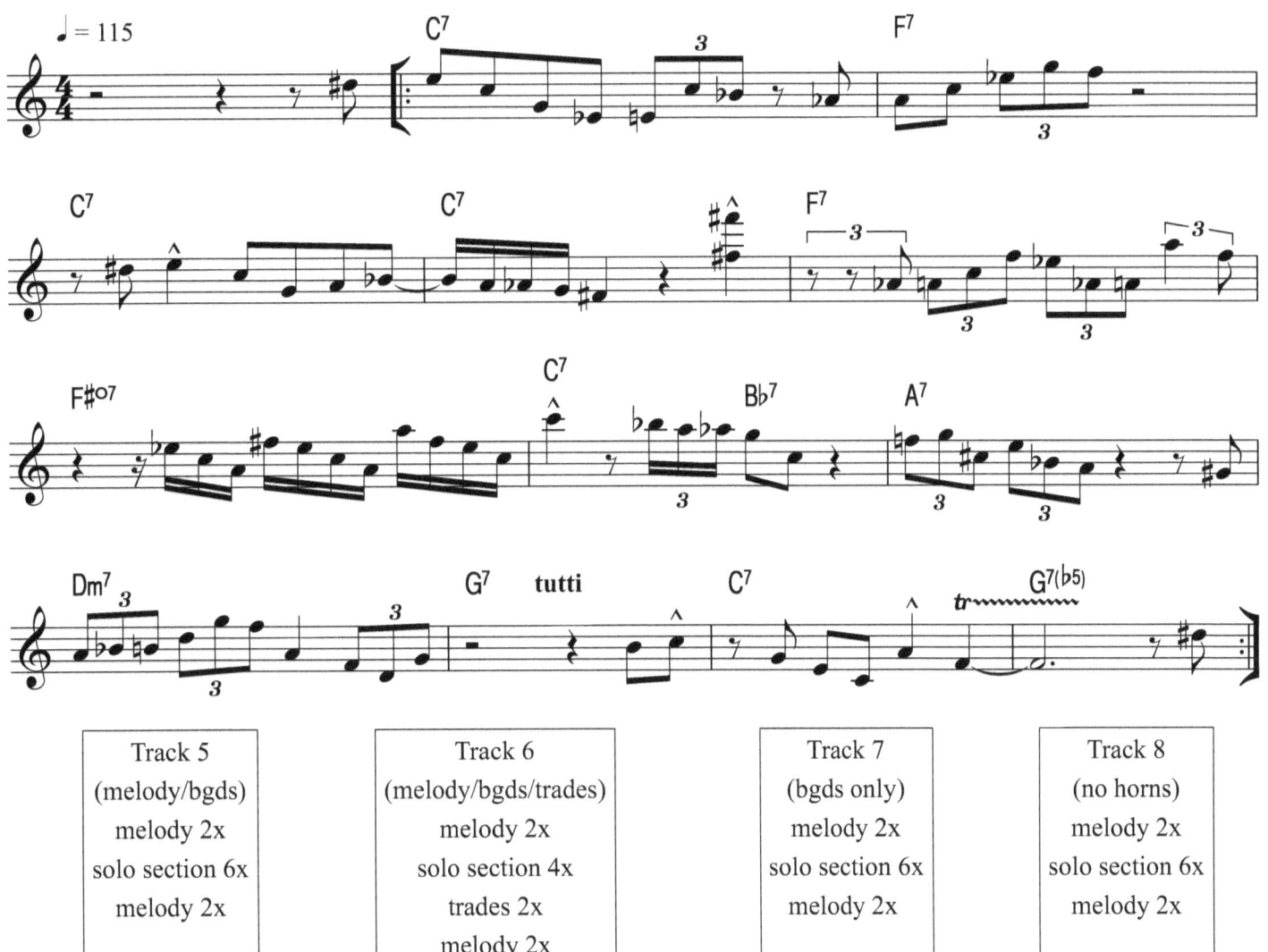

Track 5 (melody/bgds)	Track 6 (melody/bgds/trades)	Track 7 (bgds only)	Track 8 (no horns)
melody 2x	melody 2x	melody 2x	melody 2x
solo section 6x	solo section 4x	solo section 6x	solo section 6x
melody 2x	trades 2x	melody 2x	melody 2x
	melody 2x		

Track 9	Track 10	Track 11
(melody/bgds)	(bgds only)	(no horns)
melody	melody	melody
solo section (watch your repeats)	solo section (watch your repeats)	solo section (watch your repeats)
melody 1x	melody 1x	melody 1x

Trumpet in Bb (harmony) — **UNCLE SALTY** — Composed by Jeff Coffin

Track 9-Melody & BGs
Track 10-BGs
Track 11-No horns

Track 9	Track 10	Track 11
(melody/bgds)	(bgds only)	(no horns)
melody	melody	melody
solo section (watch your repeats)	solo section (watch your repeats)	solo section (watch your repeats)
melody 1x	melody 1x	melody 1x

Bb Trumpet **AL'S GREENS** Composed by Jeff Coffin

Track 12-Melody & BGs
Track 13-BGs
Track 14-No horns

intro ♩ = 100
(horns fill sparingly)

A

B
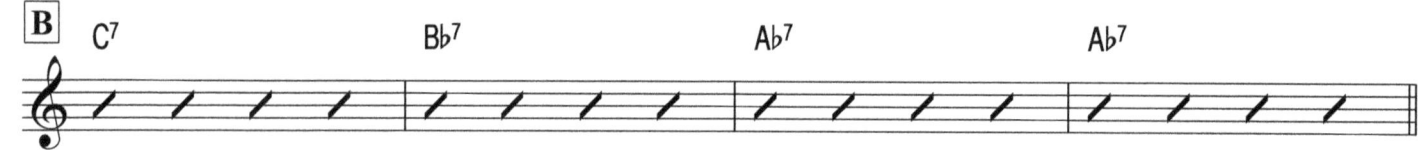

tacit melody 1st x'o
CUE THIS OUT OF SOLOS   tutti   to A for solos

slight rit. last x'o/fine

Track 12	Track 13	Track 14
(melody/bgds)	(bgds only)	(no horns)
intro	intro	intro
melody 2x	melody 2x	melody 2x
solo section (AAB) 2x	solo section (AAB) 2x	solo section (AAB) 2x
melody 1x	melody 1x	melody 1x

ESPOO YOU

Bb Trumpet
Composed by Jeff Coffin

Track 15-Melody & BGs
Track 16-Melody, BGs, Trades
Track 17-BGs
Track 18-No horns

ESPOO YOU - B♭ Trumpet

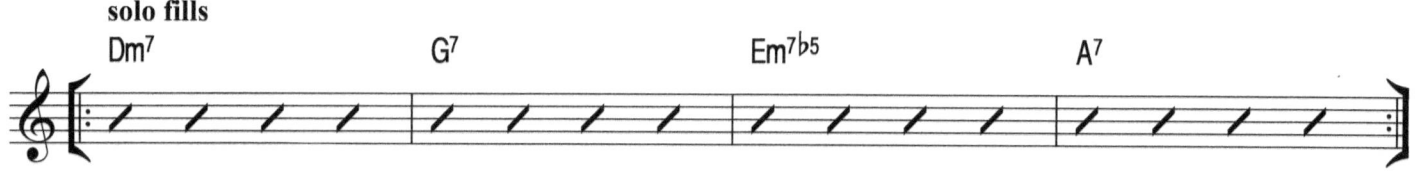

Track 15 (melody/bgds)	Track 16 (melody/bgds/trades)	Track 17 (bgds only)	Track 18 (no horns)
melody 1x	melody 1x	melody 1x	melody 1x
solo section 3x	solo section 2x	solo section 3x	solo section 3x
melody 1x	trades 1x	melody 1x	melody 1x
to coda	melody 1x	to coda	to coda
	to coda		

B♭ Trumpet (Melody) — THE MAD HATTER RIDES AGAIN — Composed by Jeff Coffin
(120 bpm)

Track 19-Melody & BGs
Track 20-BGs
Track 21-No horns

Bb Trumpet (Harmony)   **THE MAD HATTER RIDES AGAIN**   Composed by Jeff Coffin
(120 bpm)

Track 19-Melody & BGs
Track 20-BGs
Track 21-No horns

B♭ Trumpet

TALL & LANKY

Composed by Jeff Coffin

Track 26-Melody & BGs
Track 27-BGs
Track 28-No horns

*play every time behind solos

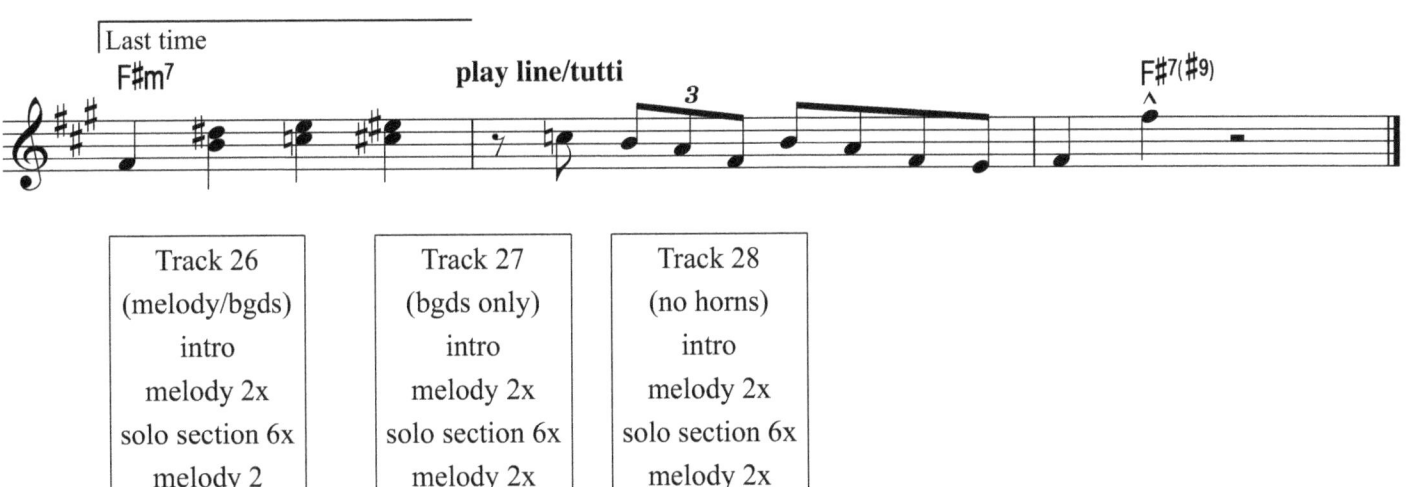

B♭ Trumpet (Harmony) **THE MAD HATTER RIDES AGAIN** Composed by Jeff Coffin
(137 bpm)

Track 29-Melody & BGs
Track 30-BGs
Track 31-No horns

4   MAD HATTER-B♭ Trumpet (Harmony)

Bb Trumpet — MOVE YOUR RUG — Composed by Jeff Coffin

Track 34-Melody & BGs
Track 35-Melody, BGs, Trades
Track 36-BGs
Track 37-No horns

NOLA second line drum intro ♩ = 196

full ryhthm section in...

A little bit about the tunes…

1. COME ON UP: Medium swing/New Orleans-ish. Quirky angular melody.

2. A JOE JONES: Blues in Bb. Horizontal and vertical melodic melody. Medium slow swing.

3. UNCLE SALTY: Folky Ornette Coleman-ish. Lots of space in the melody. Medium swing.

4. AL'S GREENS: Slow, moody, greasy and bluesy. Inspired by tenor saxophone great Joe Henderson.

5. ESPOO YOU: Medium soulful, bluesy swing / inspired by hearing Sonny Rollins in Espoo, Finland when I was there with the Bela Fleck & the Flecktones many years ago.

6. THE MAD HATTER RIDES AGAIN: One of our most popular Mu'tet tunes! Time signature of 17/8 (or, if you prefer, 8 1/2. Or 4/4, 3/4, 3/8) Done in the slower of 2 tempos (120 bpm) so you can hear and feel the odd metered groove easier. I tend to think of it as 4 quarter notes, 3 quarter notes and then 3 eighth notes. HAVE FUN!

7. STEPPIN' UP: A fun and angular melody over the changes to John Coltrane's Giant Steps - but we added a modal bridge to give it some breath and space. Oh, and the groove is like a New Orleans Brass Band! WHAT!?!

8. TALL & LANKY: Another New Orleans inspired blues with a couple bars of 7/4 for good measure over the V7 and IV7 chords. Listen for the landmark over those chords as well. It's in the 'people's key' of E minor concert.

9. THE MAD HATTER RIDES AGAIN: Time signature of 17/8 (or 8 1/2 or 4/4 3/4 3/8) Done in the faster of 2 tempos (137 bpm), this version is bumpin'! 2 solo sections!

10. SWEET MAGNOLIAS: Soulful ballad / fun and pretty easy changes.

11. MOVE YOUR RUG: New Orleans Second Line groove that is one of our favorites to play and another of our most popular tunes.

*Many of my tunes have what i call 'landmarks' that occur in them. This is to provide something 'familiar' to the listeners and players as we solo. Landmarks are important cues within the music and involve the horns more than just the basic: *'we play the melody - wait, wait, wait - play a solo - wait, wait, wait - we play the melody out and we're done.'* That's a boring cycle to me! It's easy to 'drift off' when you have nothing to play. These landmarks help remedy that by re-engaging the horn players consistently within the form of the tune.

www.ingramcontent.com/pod-product-compliance
Lightning Source LLC
Chambersburg PA
CBHW061155010526
44118CB00027B/2984